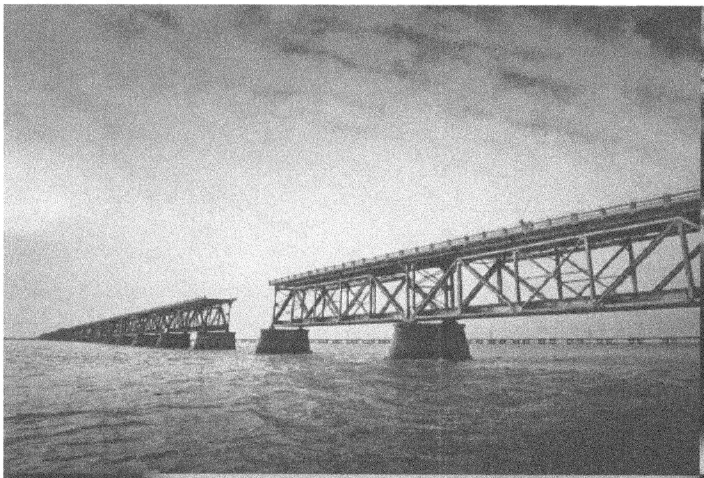

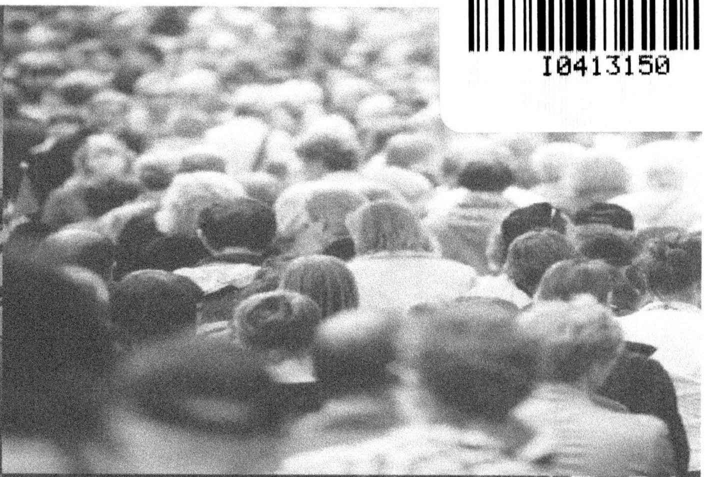

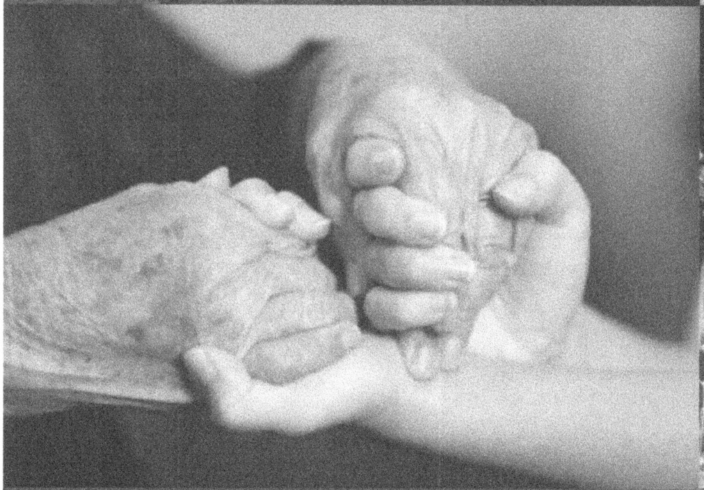

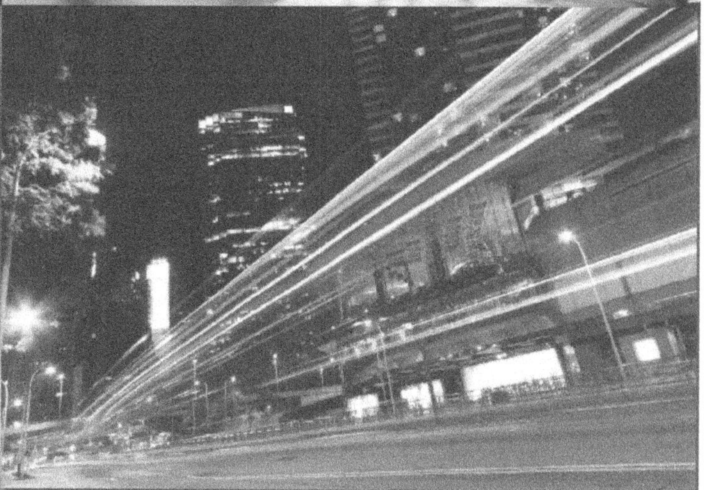

Crisis Response and Disaster Resilience 2030:

Forging Strategic Action in an Age of Uncertainty

Progress Report Highlighting the 2010-2011 Insights
of the Strategic Foresight Initiative

January 2012

The Strategic Foresight Initiative (SFI) project was coordinated by FEMA in conjunction with the emergency management community writ large. The views expressed in this report are a synthesis of the work and learning of all involved.

A special thanks to the United States Coast Guard for use of their work with scenario planning. USCG made available its newly developed *Project Evergreen* scenarios as a resource for the SFI to expand upon.

MESSAGE FROM THE FEMA OFFICE OF POLICY AND PROGRAM ANALYSIS DIRECTOR

The emergency management community faces a future with challenges likely to be far different from those we confront today. Powerful drivers of change such as globalization, technological development, and the changing roles of individuals in society have real potential to reshape the context within which we will operate. Addressing these transformations will be challenging; confronting the complexity that arises from the interaction of multiple drivers – such as demographic shifts, technology, environmental changes, and economic uncertainty – will require entirely new approaches, tools, and capabilities.

Public safety, public security, and disaster management organizations have already taken some steps to address these emerging challenges. However, the increasing pace and complexity of change calls for inclusive engagement and action so that we can proactively plan for and address shifting trends together, as a community of practice. To do this requires the emergency management community to *establish and maintain a foresight capability*. Foresight does not promote a singular vision or prediction. Instead, it considers a broad spectrum of plausible outcomes to help inform decision-making under uncertain conditions.

The Federal Emergency Management Agency (FEMA) established the Strategic Foresight Initiative (SFI) to address this need. This initiative has brought together a wide cross-section of the emergency management community to explore key future issues, trends and other factors, and to work through their implications. Working collaboratively and with urgency, we are beginning to understand the full range of changes we could encounter and the nature of our future needs; and we can begin to execute a shared agenda for action.

This report presents the findings from foresight efforts thus far, including: uncertainties that define and drive the future environment; strategic needs and gaps our community will have to address; a look into the emergency management community of 2030; and finally, suggested next steps for the community to prepare for the future. The strategic needs in particular – grouped into Essential Capabilities, Innovative Models and Tools, and Dynamic Partnerships – are intended as a catalyst for leaders throughout the emergency management community to prepare themselves and the Nation for the challenges and opportunities the future holds.

The products of this foresight initiative are offered as a starting point for dialogue and active consideration throughout the emergency management community. The thoughts and ideas presented in this report do not encompass all of the nuances and situations we will meet in the future. Rather, they offer a foundation for developing a shared understanding of potential future challenges and how, working together, we may address these challenges.

The work of the SFI is not possible without the participation of many dedicated professionals from across the United States, spanning many fields and disciplines, as well as our international colleagues. These contributions have already generated tremendous knowledge and insight, and will carry this work forward to meet our shared future demands.

David J. Kaufman

Director, FEMA Office of Policy and Program Analysis

This Page Left Intentionally Blank

TABLE OF CONTENTS

Message from the FEMA Office of Policy and Program Analysis Director i

List of Acronyms and Definitions iv

I. **Introduction to the Strategic Foresight Initiative** 1

    Overview and Purpose 1

    A Guidepost to Understanding Our Future Landscape 2

    The SFI Process and Report Structure 3

II. **Exploring Forces of Change** 6

    Social and Technological Drivers 7

    Environmental Driver 8

    Economic and Political Drivers 9

III. **Identifying Strategic Needs** 11

    The SFI Scenario Workshop 12

    Essential Capabilities 13

    Innovative Models & Tools 15

    Dynamic Partnerships 18

IV. **A Future Glimpse into Emergency Management** 21

    Essential Capabilities in 2030 21

    Innovative Models and Tools in 2030 22

    Dynamic Partnerships in 2030 22

V. **The Way Forward** 24

Appendix A–The SFI Process 26

    Environmental Scanning 26

    Scenario Planning 29

    Advancing and Sustaining Strategic Foresight 31

Appendix B–SFI Drivers 32

    Social and Technological Drivers: 32

    Environmental Driver: 33

    Economic and Political Drivers: 33

Appendix C – SFI Participating Organizations 35

LIST OF ACRONYMS AND DEFINITIONS

DHS	United States Department of Homeland Security
DNI	United States Director of National Intelligence
Driver	Forces of change that will individually and collectively shape the future environment in unpredictable ways
Emergency Management	The field of practice responsible for preparing for, preventing, protecting against, mitigating the effects of, responding to, and recovering from all threats and hazards.
Emergency Management Community	The broad community of practice involved in emergency management. This community includes, but is not limited to the following: traditional state, local, federal, and tribal emergency managers; those in public security, public health, and public safety agencies; first responders; public works; business partners; non-governmental organizations (NGOs); federal agencies with equities in emergency management; and academicians who have studied or published on the topic of emergency management.
FEMA	Federal Emergency Management Agency
NGO	Non-Governmental Organization
NIC	United States National Intelligence Council
Strategic Action	Those actions taken to meet future strategic needs
SFI	Strategic Foresight Initiative
Strategic Need	The capabilities, tools, partnerships, and other resources emergency managers would need to be successful in future operating environments
USCG	United States Coast Guard

I. INTRODUCTION TO THE STRATEGIC FORESIGHT INITIATIVE

Overview and Purpose

As the emergency management community[1] looks toward 2030, one thing is certain – the world will not look the same as it does today. Shifting demographics and the rate of technological innovation will challenge the way we plan and communicate with the public. Constraints on spending at all levels—federal, state, local, and tribal—are forcing and will continue to force us to rethink what activities we can truly afford to do and how to build partnerships to accomplish our objectives. At the same time, more frequent and more intense storms will present operational challenges and complexities. Any of these issues alone would challenge some current emergency management policies and procedures. In combination, these and other forces of change produce a difficult, highly uncertain future, the complexity of which will test the ability of the emergency management community to execute our mission. Exploring the nature of such future challenges can help us take actions to improve our Nation's resilience and adaptability.

Launched in 2010, the Strategic Foresight Initiative (SFI) is a transformative, community-wide effort to create an enduring foresight capability. It is intended to advance strategic planning and thinking about the future, to prepare the community both for emerging challenges and for the key opportunities presented by our changing environment. Its core focus is to understand the factors driving change in our world, and to analyze how they will impact the emergency management field in the United States over the next 20 years. Thinking more broadly, rigorously, and over a longer timeframe will help us:

- Hedge against uncertainty;
- Avoid strategic surprises;
- Promote information sharing across disciplines and organizations;
- Understand what changes could affect emergency management; and
- Prepare and plan to more effectively operate in our future environment.

Fundamentally, the SFI seeks two outcomes: (1) an emergency management community prepared for whatever challenges the future holds; and (2) a common sense of direction and urgency, to drive action toward meeting our shared future needs—starting today. Achieving these objectives will require ongoing conversations among diverse stakeholders, the creation of a common sense of

---

[1] **Emergency Management**: The field of practice responsible for preparing for, preventing, protecting against, mitigating the effects of, responding to, and recovering from all threats and hazards.

Emergency Management Community: The broad community of practice involved in emergency management. This community includes, but is not limited to the following: traditional state, local, federal, and tribal emergency managers; those in public security, public health, and public safety agencies; first responders; public works; business partners; non-governmental organizations (NGOs); federal agencies with equities in emergency management; and academicians who have studied or published on the topic of emergency management.

Strategic
Foresight Initiative

1

awareness, and leadership throughout the community to make the needed changes to prepare our Nation for the future.

This report is intended to provide planners and managers with insights that can shape a range of critical decisions, starting *today*. Such decisions—which can be made in advance of disasters—include improving prioritization of resources and investments, managing new and unfamiliar risks, forging new partnerships, and understanding emerging legal and regulatory hurdles.

A Guidepost to Understanding Our Future Landscape

The SFI explored forces of change (i.e., drivers), plausible future operating conditions, challenges, and opportunities, and was designed to identify what the emergency management community would need to be successful, regardless of what the future holds. Throughout the process, as we gained more knowledge and discussed ideas and thoughts, we continued to ask: How has our view of the future changed? Have we missed anything critical? What are the secondary and tertiary implications of what we have found? What have been significant and recurring ideas time and again? Pondering these questions resulted in a number of insights, high-level observations to inform and guide decision-makers in the more immediate term. These insights are a set of recurring themes or conditions that we should consider as we build actions to meet our future needs. They are not intended as predictions of how the future will unfold; rather, they are intended to serve as a lens through which to view our future landscape and the actions we as a community will need to take to be successful.

As stated throughout this document, the emergency management community faces ***increasing complexity and decreasing predictability in its operating environment***. Complexity will take the form of more incidents, new and unfamiliar threats, more information to analyze (possibly with less time to process it), new players and participants, sophisticated technologies, and exceedingly high public expectations. This combination will create a vastly different landscape for risk assessment and operational planning. Pressure to perform in this environment will be extraordinary.

One of the major areas of uncertainty surrounds the ***evolving needs of at-risk populations***. As U.S. demographics change, we will have to plan to serve increasing numbers of elderly and limited and non-English speaking citizens; the possibility of massive numbers of pandemic victims; physically isolated populations (by choice, or because of some form of disaster); technology have-nots; migratory populations inside and outside our borders; and large numbers of homeless or destitute people, among others. It will be crucial to engage these communities as future challenges strain our community's resources and capabilities.

Future resource constraints are seemingly unavoidable, at least for the foreseeable future. Whether they are induced by an increased need for services, a reduced capability or capacity to deliver services, or both, we will be faced with limited funding for emergency management. These constraints will push service providers to find creative ways to deal with shortfalls. This underlines

the need for innovative new surge models, new partnerships, and sustained community efforts to ensure interoperability of personnel, equipment, systems, and functions.

Inevitably, in this kind of environment, ***individuals, families, neighborhoods, communities, and the private sector will likely play an increasingly active role*** in meeting emergency management needs. The public's ability and desire to self-organize will grow, as the role of the individual, access to information, and technology all evolve.

Meanwhile, ***disparities in fiscal resources and in access to advanced technology, to know-how, to skilled personnel, etc.*** will have to be anticipated and effectively managed. Wealthier states with stronger infrastructure and better-educated populations will be in a more advantageous position to deal with disasters and emergencies than poorer ones.

The nation will benefit from expansive thinking about these issues. Our global relationships contain both important challenges (e.g., supply chain risks) and opportunities (e.g., partnerships, force multipliers, and new approaches). Indeed, beyond U.S. experience, there is ***a large and growing body of global best practices*** from which we can learn and benefit.

Finally, ***the importance of trust – between the public and government*** – cannot be overstated, especially since belief in large institutions, including government, has been shifting to social networks and alternative sources of loyalty. This shift poses real challenges to emergency management, especially in the face of changing political expectations and greater public awareness of government limitations. Since trust is so essential to successful outcomes in disasters and emergencies, we must look for opportunities to build and strengthen public trust. Frequently the best pathway for doing so lies in ever wider and deeper channels of public participation.

Recognizing these observations and the complexities they present, we have the opportunity to create roadmaps for the development of realistic capabilities, models, tools, and partnerships to fulfill our future needs.

The SFI Process and Report Structure

The SFI adopted a rigorous approach to thinking about future needs for emergency management (Appendix A documents the full extent of the SFI process). This report represents the most comprehensive analysis to date of the future outlook facing those in our community of practice. Based on the outputs of a robust and collaborative futures-planning process, the report provides a framework for understanding how the operating environment for emergency management is apt to change in the coming decades.

This report covers key SFI findings to date:

- An examination of the *forces of change* shaping the emergency management world;
- An identification of vital and compelling *strategic needs* suggested by exploration of alternative emergency management scenarios; and

- An image of future emergency management capacities and capabilities—if we are successful in meeting the challenges the future will present.

An initial review of current news, social science, and technology literature helped identify an expansive range of important trends and drivers that would shape the future operating environment. This foundation was followed by in-depth discussions with thought leaders on key trends, and multiple structured stakeholder engagement sessions with many representatives of the emergency management community. The results of this work are described in Section II.

A singular, isolated focus on drivers, however, would not yield a complete picture of future emergency management conditions. The effects of drought over the next five years, for example, are easier to project than a more uncertain 20-year timeframe. Technological solutions, such as desalinization, could be the solution to droughts. Or, alternatively, the crisis could be exacerbated by extreme fiscal distress. Both possibilities are plausible and must be considered.

To deal with the complexities and uncertainties inherent in any future outlook, the SFI used scenario planning to provide a framework for deeper exploration. Built on the driver analysis, scenario planning allowed the community to examine various driver cross-impacts and imagine the influence unknown variables could have on future operating environments. While not intended to be predictive of what the future holds, scenario planning offers a robust structure for thinking about alternative—and plausible—future operating environments.

Section III highlights the scenarios developed for the SFI exercise to consider an expansive range of social, political, economic, regulatory, environmental, and technological conditions in the future. This section also synthesizes the results of an in-depth exploration of the strategic implications of the five SFI scenarios—ultimately identifying 15 *strategic needs* for the emergency management community. These strategic needs identify what the emergency management community would need to be successful in future environments – needs that should inform priorities, investments and decisions on the part of emergency managers.

Section IV helps to illustrate how the identified strategic needs translate into practice by imagining the emergency management community of the future in 2030—playing out a storyline of the community that succeeded in meeting those 15 strategic needs. Finally, Section V provides an outlook of the way forward, outlining ideas for SFI activities in 2012 and beyond.

The findings in this report capture the results of an extensive community-wide effort that has benefited from the contributions of more than 800 professionals, academics, and interested parties from all layers of the public and private sector. As you read this report, consider it a framework for understanding how the operating environment for emergency management is apt to change over the next few decades. Although we have begun addressing our future needs, our progress is not enough. We must do more. To build a more resilient, adaptive and proactive emergency

management community, we must approach the future with urgency, and we must increase our pace of change. We hope that this report fosters the necessary conversations and ideas to do just that.

II. EXPLORING FORCES OF CHANGE

Today's strategic environment is defined by, among other characteristics, borderless and unconventional threats, global challenges, and long-term trends. In an age of increasing complexity and uncertainty, there are many forces of change, or "drivers," reshaping our world. To begin exploring what drivers could most significantly shape the future of emergency management, the SFI employed an analytical framework used commonly by organizations such as the U.S. National Intelligence Council (NIC), to identify macro-level factors that have significant influence in the world. These factors fall into five dimensions – Social, Technological, Environmental, Economic, and Political (STEEP). Changes in these dimensions will complicate the future emergency management environment, significantly alter how members of the emergency management community perform our jobs in the future, and require creative and collaborative thinking and action.

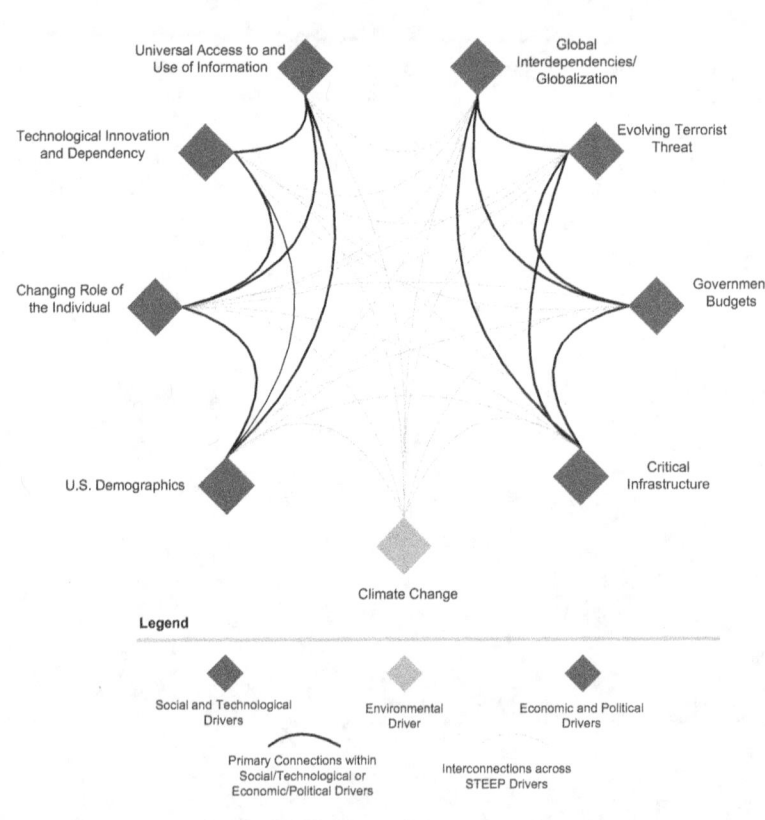

Figure 1: SFI drivers interconnection map

Representatives from across the emergency management community participated in the SFI effort to examine a wide spectrum of forces of change, and to date have identified nine key drivers that are particularly influential. Research[2], subject matter expertise, and rigorous scenario-planning methods highlight that these nine drivers will individually and collectively shape the future in unpredictable ways, creating an increasingly complex world full of new challenges and opportunities. This section represents the SFI's synthesized analysis of these nine drivers' potential impacts.

---

[2] The majority of the driver research in Section II comes from the SFI driver papers (links found in Appendix B) and is therefore not cited. Research not found in the SFI driver papers is otherwise footnoted in this report.

Strategic Foresight Initiative

Social and Technological Drivers

Major social and technological trends—specifically, *Universal Access to and Use of Information, Technological Innovation and Dependency*, the *Changing Role of the Individual,* and *Shifting U.S. Demographics*—will have profound impacts on the future. Rapid innovations in technology are transforming media and communication, altering how people interact with each other and relate to society and institutions. While emergency managers will have new capabilities in the future, the people who rely on their services will have different needs and expectations, requiring new pathways for engaging diverse communities and building greater resilience to disasters throughout the Nation.

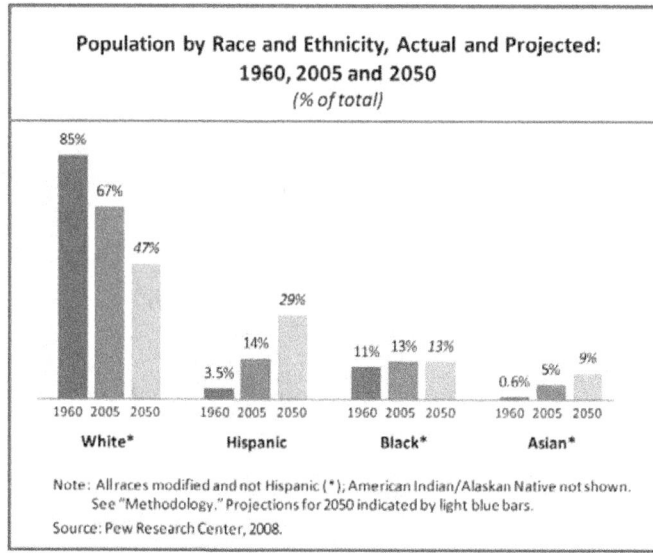

Figure 2. Population by Race and Ethnicity, Actual and Projected: 1960, 2005 and 2050

The pace of technological change—from biotechnology and nanotechnology to information and communication technology—is accelerating and affecting nearly every facet of life. Smart phones, high-speed internet, and "cloud" computing, to name only a few examples, are transforming how people do business, communicate, and carry out essential services such as health care. But the increased pervasiveness of technology is exposing new risks: dependence on computer systems to manage operations in multiple sectors, such as water, telecommunications, and transportation infrastructure, increases systemic vulnerabilities, including the threat of cyber-attacks.

Furthermore, technological innovation and the public's evolving expectations of government are fundamentally altering how individuals interact with society—leading to a redefinition of community. It is increasingly clear that there are many different kinds of communities, including communities of place, interest, belief, and circumstance, which can exist both geographically and virtually. Along with the changing profile of communities, new tools empower the public to play a greater role in identifying "what matters" and producing content themselves. In addition, evolving patterns of information flow have changed the role of the media and modes of information exchange. The explosion of social media and personal communications technology will continue to increase real-time access and delivery of information. Public access to "raw" data sources, such as Data.gov, expands the possibilities of how existing information can be used, and increases expectations of government transparency.

The U.S. population is growing, aging significantly, and becoming more ethnically diverse. These are transformative trends: by 2025, as immigration continues to fuel the majority of population growth (with foreign-born residents projected to reach historic highs of roughly 15 percent of the population[3]), nearly 1 in 5 Americans will be older than 65. Moreover, people are residing in more densely populated urban and coastal areas. Higher concentrations of people and assets in these areas (with over 200 million in "metro areas" and 87 million living along U.S. coastlines) may increase the Nation's vulnerability to impacts from severe weather.

Environmental Driver

While there are various environmental stressors that deeply affect society, such as pollution, ecosystem degradation and resource depletion, and diminishing fresh water supplies, *Climate Change* is the major environmental force confronting the emergency management community in the United States. Climate change impacts are expected to increase the severity, frequency, or scale of extreme weather events, droughts, floods, sea-level rise, precipitation patterns, and the spread of life-threatening diseases. The most visible impacts will likely result from an increase in the magnitude and frequency of natural disasters, which will affect the resilience of local communities and the operational demands placed on emergency management systems.

Climate change can affect core emergency management mission areas and our long-term vision of reducing physical and

Woodstock, Vt., September 4, 2011 -- Tropical storm Irene caved in many roads after dropping more than 11 inches of rain. This caused floods which destroyed much of Vermont's infrastructure. Photo by Wendell A. Davis Jr.

Figure 3. Woodstock, VT, September 4, 2011

economic loss from disasters in three primary ways: (1) impacts on mitigation, preparedness, response, and recovery operations, (2) resiliency of critical infrastructure and various emergency assets; and (3) triggering indirect impacts—population displacement, migration, public health risks among them—that increase mission risks.

---

[3] Population projections of immigrant families and foreign-born residents are provided by a 2008 Pew Research Center report, "U.S. population projections 2005-2050."
Source: http://pewhispanic.org/files/reports/85.pdf

Economic and Political Drivers

The environment in which we operate is increasingly defined by countervailing economic and political forces: continuing globalization, increasing interdependencies in governance institutions and business, and limited economic growth in the industrialized world that are constraining government budgets and creating resource limitations. In this environment, as businesses and governments rely on interlinked global supply chains, critical infrastructure in the U.S. is deteriorating, and the global balance of power is shifting toward "emerging markets." Compounding these drivers is the evolving terrorist threat: terrorist organizations continue to plot attacks while inciting and radicalizing small groups and individuals to target America, its interests, aspirations, and way of life. Collectively, these four key economic and political drivers—*Global Interdependencies/Globalization*, *Government Budgets*, *Critical Infrastructure*, and the *Evolving Terrorist Threat*—will have significant impacts on the future of emergency management.

Christchurch, New Zealand, February 25, 2011 -- Tim Manning, left, Deputy Administrator for Protection and National Preparedness at the Federal Emergency Management Agency, inspecting earthquake damage in Christchurch. Manning was in Christchurch attending a U.S.-N.Z. Partnership Forum when the earthquake struck. FEMA/U.S. Embassy-New Zealand/Janine Burns

Figure 4: Christchurch, New Zealand, February 25, 2011

In recent decades, economic growth in developing countries has lifted millions out of poverty while creating new global interdependencies based on trade and commerce. Although improved living standards in some places may yield greater community resilience to disasters, inadequate institutional capacity in other places, and deepening regional ties, may result in greater demand for U.S. assistance in international disaster relief. Moreover, America's reliance on an increasingly vulnerable global supply chain and shifting international power dynamics may also mean that catastrophes abroad have a greater impact domestically. The availability of technological and scientific knowledge has the potential to transform both terrorist and counterterrorist capabilities. Global terrorist organizations are adopting new tactics (e.g., cyber terrorism), while the threat of homegrown terrorist activity continues to grow. This is compounded by near- and medium-term economic forecasts that show serious budget constraints at all levels of government. Diminished resources, increasing health care costs, and the costs of retirement benefits will have direct and indirect impacts at all levels of government for years to come. In the private and public sectors, aging transportation, communication, energy, and health care infrastructure pose significant threats and are in danger of failing over the next 20 years. Collapsing bridges, bursting water mains, cascading brownouts from a fragile power grid, and overburdened health and medical

Strategic Foresight Initiative

systems are all examples of this well-documented situation. Without reliable infrastructure in place, protection, response, and recovery operations may suffer.

Developing a broad and comprehensive understanding of these drivers of change provides a foundation for knowing what the emergency management community needs to do to address emerging challenges or take advantage of opportunities. While these nine drivers are not the only potential forces of change, any one of them alone may challenge some emergency management policies and procedures. In combination, these and other significant developments may converge to trigger dramatic change, which would likely test the readiness and resilience of the emergency management system as it exists today.

III. IDENTIFYING STRATEGIC NEEDS

It is important to appreciate that while each driver can be a catalyst for change by itself, much of its transformative impact on how we live and work will come from intersections with other drivers. Scenario planning offered the SFI the opportunity to play out varying driver conditions – and driver cross-impacts – in alternative operating "worlds," allowing for a range of driver effects and impacts to be explored. This in turn allowed for the identification of strategic needs – the capabilities, tools, partnerships, etc. the emergency management community would need to successfully fulfill its mission no matter how the future transpires.

The SFI used a set of five distinct scenarios that allowed the nine identified drivers in Section II to be fully characterized in all their complexity and uncertain future end-states. This set of scenarios addressed a wide variety of conditions which these drivers could present to us, both individually and in concert.

As depicted in the table below, for example, in the "Bet on the Wrong Horse" scenario, the trend toward extreme weather has stalled, suggesting a possible end to climate change. But the U.S. has already invested significant resources to deal with global warming and is now suffering substantial economic consequences. On the other end of the climate spectrum, in a different scenario, "Quantum Leap," the U.S. (and much of the world) has been hard hit by extreme weather and climatic conditions. Technological solutions have mitigated the worst effects, but not completely, and not evenly across the nation.

Similarly, the "Treading Water" scenario presents a U.S. economy in its worst shape since the Great Depression. Families and communities are experiencing significant and prolonged decline in living standards while the U.S. has become much more isolationist. The economic situation is not quite so dire in the "Dude, Where's My Sovereignty" scenario, but the nation has still not addressed long-term fiscal challenges, and the U.S. has lost its global competitiveness. In contrast, in the "Dragon vs. Tiger" scenario the U.S. once again boasts a relatively strong, vibrant and globally-integrated economy. In this scenario the U.S. has made up for many lost years of deleveraging. Instead of debt and jobs, as in other scenarios, the major political concerns in "Dragon vs. Tiger" surround the rising potential for nuclear confrontation between Asia's two rising powers.

The table below provides a sample of how each scenario addressed the range of drivers. Appendix A includes high-level narrative descriptions of each scenario world.

SELECT SFI SCENARIO CHARACTERISTICS

(abbreviated list)

Scenario — Scenario Characteristic	Quantum Leap	Bet on the Wrong Horse	Dragon vs Tiger	Treading Water	Dude, Where's My Sovereignty?
US Economy	Strong, vibrant, dynamic	Lethargic, in and out of recessions	Strong rebound after a period of decline and	Worst since Great Depression	Lagging peer competitors
Climate & Weather	Extreme events more frequent	Stabilizing; climate change possibly reversed	Steady state trend in climate change	Worsening trend, with more extreme weather	More severe storms, droughts and flooding.
Infrastructure	Bleeding-edge modernization underway	Mixed; transport lags global trends	Highly advanced, with embedded IT and security	Seriously degraded	General decline; pay-per-use is widespread
States & Localities	Relatively strong, but with pockets of distress	Rural areas hit by population shifts to urban areas	Recovering after massive federal bail-outs	Extreme fiscal vulnerability with paring of fed help	States very powerful but prospects vary
Major Threat Areas	Climate change effects, technology in wrong hands	Cyber-security, chronic fiscal pressures	Potential for nuclear conflict abroad; complacency	Pandemics, poverty, limited public resources	Underfunded entitlements; foreign influence; weak federal leadership

THE SFI SCENARIO WORKSHOP

In July 2011 a representative group of nearly 60 members of the emergency management community participated in a unique four-day scenario workshop. During this exercise, each participant was immersed in one of the five SFI scenarios. The job of each group was to understand threats, challenges, and opportunities its scenario world contained, and from this analysis draft a set of strategic needs that would be important for the emergency management community to address in that particular scenario. The strategic needs generated by all five groups were compared and evaluated to determine which strategic needs applied across all scenario worlds.

The SFI Scenario Workshop yielded a set of 15 common strategic needs that applied across all five scenario worlds – capacities, capabilities or enabling prerequisites the community would need to be successful in the future, no matter how the future actually turned out. Three high-level categories of needs emerged in extensive post-workshop analysis: (1) **Essential Capabilities** the community will need to build or enhance in order to meet future challenges; (2) **Innovative Models and Tools** emergency managers will need to optimize resources, anticipate events, or deal with complex and/or unprecedented problems; and (3) **Dynamic Partnerships** that will need to be formed or strengthened to meet surge requirements or to absorb critical new skills and capabilities.

The 15 common strategic needs, organized by category, are described below.

ESSENTIAL CAPABILITIES

Through the SFI process we have learned that blisteringly rapid change and complexity will define the emergency management environment over the next few decades. Even demographics, here in the U.S. traditionally one of the more slow-moving and predictable trends, could be subject to sudden and unpredictable lurches, in the face of climate change, pandemic outbreaks, refugee surges or some other factor not even considered today. Meanwhile, new service challenges are arising as government agencies – from Washington down to the smallest towns – wrestle with new responsibilities and extremely challenging fiscal conditions. All of this is playing out in a data-rich but often knowledge-poor environment, where nearly everyone is an information consumer, contributor, and critic.

Not surprisingly, these dynamics will drive demand for new, augmented, or otherwise different emergency management capabilities. Several of the suggested capabilities highlighted during the July 2011 SFI scenario workshop are explained below.

1. Develop emergency management capabilities to address dynamic and unprecedented shifts in local and regional population characteristics and migratory flows. Among other things, this could include building multi-lingual proficiencies and understanding risks associated with both heavily populated coastal areas and urban centers and more remote locations where new population centers are forming. This will require close dialogue with community leaders to better understand local needs, including new vulnerable populations and emergency operating challenges related to issues like aging infrastructure. And it will mean involving traditionally underrepresented populations in planning and service delivery.

Why this need? Emergency managers will be faced with complex demographics shifts as the United States' population increases, ages, and becomes more culturally and linguistically diverse. New challenges will arise from migrations within the U.S., possibly because of environmental issues and changes in regional climates. There will also be changes in the size and nature of traditionally underrepresented and elusive populations, including the extremely poor; the homeless; those volunteering to live "off the grid"; refugees from disasters; and victims of pandemics.

---

2. Practice omni-directional knowledge sharing. This means employing all relevant forums, networks (including sensitive and classified), and technologies so that information created and distributed by government remains relevant to the public in complex information and media environments. And it will mean staying abreast of the rapidly evolving world of social networks and knowing how to leverage their power and influence.

Why this need? The proliferation of information from all sources (including private sector and social media) intensifies the need to make emergency management information and knowledge useful and

13

accessible. Advanced tools to collect, analyze and disseminate information represent potentially valuable new tools for emergency managers. As information flows become more widely distributed, the connectivity of networks will be significantly more important than any single hierarchical solution. And the public's role as an information source will be vital.

---

3. Infuse emergency management principles and life skills across the entire educational experience to empower individuals to assume more responsibility. This means continuing to build emergency management awareness, from K through 12, with community-tailored curricula shaped by the local environment. It is about communicating the importance of partnering with individuals and community organizations to build self-reliance and individual initiative.

Why this need? Future operating environments may well be characterized by significant decline in governmental resources for emergency management. Such fiscal constraints could tempt emergency managers to pull back from community engagement, which would widen the gap that already exists. Instead, it will be important to use the fiscal environment as an opportunity to reinvent and innovate. Schools and youth programs will be critically important channels, especially in creating awareness of new and unfamiliar threats such as pandemics or cyber attacks.

---

4. Build a shared vision for the emergency management community of the future and a culture that embraces forward thinking to anticipate emerging challenges and develops appropriate plans and contingencies. This might include building "futures" knowledge and insights into operational and leadership training, examining and adopting global best practices, or exploring the development of an emergency management academy that has a foresight component.

Why this need? The SFI scenarios depict increasingly complex, rapidly changing worlds – even for economically troubled and less technologically vibrant scenarios. Since current operational strategies and plans may not be applicable in the future, the emergency management community will have to deliberately explore future issues as it prepares for the challenges that face our community.

5. Leverage volunteer capabilities across all emergency management phases. This need is about creatively incorporating volunteers into our operating models – and dealing with the non-trivial risks involved, particularly in supervision, training, and liability. Technology may come to play an important role in volunteer organization and training.

North Sioux City, S.D., June 12, 2011 -- These Upward Bound students from Rosebud and Pine Ridge, SD communities are filling sandbags for residents to use in an effort to prevent damage from along the Missouri River.

Figure 5: North Sioux City, S.D., June 12, 2011

Why this need? Emergency management resources, especially personnel, are apt to be stretched in future operating environments marked by tight budgets and/or more frequent national emergencies. In some cases, skill gaps may become more pronounced, and alternative staffing models will become important. How might we further incorporate volunteers into our operating models? What limitations must we understand to mitigate undue risk exposure? Further, even though it is already used to mobilize communities, how can we better use technology to inform and organize volunteers?

INNOVATIVE MODELS & TOOLS

Foresight tells us that the future will challenge us to be even more inventive in our thinking about the tools and solutions we will need to be successful. For one, we expect that the future operating environment will be characterized by more frequent emergency events, many of which will be simultaneous. In addition, these events are apt to have more far-reaching impacts, simply because the world is more complex, networked, and interdependent. Combined with aging infrastructure, potential supply chain risks, and technological advancements, our environment becomes even more difficult to navigate. Thus, we will need to employ, and in some cases develop, new and improved models and tools to successfully meet our critical missions.

SFI scenario workshop participants identified tremendous opportunities in the Innovative Models & Tools category. Related Strategic Needs that proved effective across scenario worlds are explained below.

6. Adopt new risk management tools and processes in order to manage cascading consequences of interactions among infrastructure and all hazards. Emergency managers will need advanced modeling and tools to prospectively assess and manage risks related to climate, power, transport, telecommunications, and water, among other domains. Additionally,

Strategic Foresight Initiative

understanding and remediating potential points of catastrophic failure will be important. And as populations shift we will have to plan more appropriately to provide services to the public.

Why this need? Current risk management tools and processes already are outdated. For example, our risk management models are typically retrospective and do not account for climate change impacts we are experiencing today. If climate change is exacerbated, we will be even further behind the curve, our mitigation efforts will prove insufficient, and our response and recovery operations will suffer. The risks of aging infrastructure due to budget pressures, political and jurisdictional conflicts, and potential failures to initiate or sustain the long-term investments required also will challenge us in the future. Aging infrastructure also represents a highly interconnected form of risk, with many secondary and tertiary risks to populations during and following emergency situations.

---

7. Employ alternative surge models to meet the challenging confluences of social, technological, environmental, economic, and political factors and conditions. This could include regional and sub-regional sharing of assets, infrastructure, and logistics capabilities. Considering new staffing models that include greater volunteer, private sector, non-governmental organization, and armed forces support also could help meet this need.

Why this need? Acute and possibly chronic fiscal pressure could create highly challenging deficits in emergency management resources relative to needs, and public safety and emergency management practitioners could see reduced funding at all levels. Possible offsetting factors, such as technology, could be an important force multiplier in some situations. However, all of this suggests the need for new approaches and models for marshaling resources to deal with the possibility of more frequent and more complex emergency situations.

---

8. Establish flexible frameworks that optimize emergency management inter-operability across all boundaries, because of increasing jurisdictional and technological complexities. These include, but are not limited to, medical professional licensures, communication and messaging, equipment training, and security standards. This could require comprehensive frameworks to remediate; engaging the public and private sectors will be important to ensure we are meeting differing communities' needs.

Why this need? The future operating environment will challenge individual emergency management entities to accomplish more with fewer of their own resources. This underlines the importance of resource-sharing arrangements across jurisdictions, especially during emergency situations. In 2011, doctors and nurses cannot cross state lines to help in emergencies unless a governor declares a state of emergency. Obstacles to many other forms of interoperability, including security, law enforcement, and technology, to include our hemispheric partners, will be magnified unless there is reform in this area.

9. Plan and coordinate around shared interests and interdependencies to exercise the entire range of emergency management capabilities. This will require effective leadership, which can come from multiple sources, aligning strategies and operations across sectors, and using tools such as models, scenarios, and simulations as learning opportunities to tease out stress points and gaps and address them.

Why this need? The future may challenge our community with chronic resource constraints at times of rising demands for emergency management services. Current regional approaches are limited. Planners need to be motivated and empowered to look beyond short-term concerns and narrow stovepipes and recognize opportunities for collaboration around shared interests.

10. Remediate hidden vulnerabilities in critical supplies – from water to energy to medical products –to offset threats to the full scope of emergency management activities. Having an understanding of supply chain vulnerabilities of *all* supplies, not just commodities, would benefit the emergency management community when considering future supply lines. Further, developing contingencies in anticipation of both global and local supply challenges is in our best interest.

Why this need? Future availability of important emergency supplies cannot be assured. Global and national supply chains, some of which have

Greensburg, Kan., June 29, 2011 -- This 10-turbine wind farm supplies enough clean electricity to power all the homes, businesses, and municipal facilities in Greensburg. The city is rebuilding after an EF-5 tornado destroyed 95 percent of the structures. Steve Zumwalt FEMA

Figure 6: Greensburg, Kansas, June 29, 2011

limited capacity to begin with, may be vulnerable to infrastructure degradation, interruptions in foreign trade, and cyber attacks, and they are undergoing radical structural changes in warehousing demand signaling and logistics. Water, especially in drought-stricken areas of the country, may not be available in sufficient amounts to fully support emergency management missions. Climate change may negatively affect access to power and energy; so may man-made problems, such as foreign conflicts and trade embargoes.

11. Influence the development of emerging technologies that advance emergency management capabilities. This will require sustained dialogue between the emergency management and technology communities. We will have to help technologists understand the technological requirements of emergency managers so that appropriate technologies can be developed. Ensuring technological interoperability with our stakeholders as technology evolves will also be a critical consideration.

Why this need? Technology will become a more important element in future emergency management mission execution, from information management to communications, to sensing, to transportation and logistics, and much more. In fact, there is a case to be made that technology will be even more important in tight budget environments. This argues not just for proactive technology adoption, but actually getting out ahead and influencing the development of products that have emergency management applications.

DYNAMIC PARTNERSHIPS

Partnerships are and will continue to be critical to the future of emergency management. For this community, partnerships are not merely standard operating procedures – they are essential. In an environment of fiscal constraints and changing government roles and responsibilities, the partnership imperative must rise to a whole new level, involving new associations, broader and deeper interactions, and immense fluidity.

It begins with individuals and communities. Working with communities to understand their needs, and where emergency managers can empower and assist, is a shift in approach, but it is necessary. Further, as we look to the future, businesses will continue to serve as a core member of the emergency management team, and they will be crucial to successful service delivery. We also will need to engage our international partners, in particular Canada and Mexico, around several shared interests, including border security, immigration, water management, and disease surveillance. And our partnership with the U.S. Armed Forces as we respond to and recover from complex disaster situations will benefit our collective efforts.

Strengthening (and, in some cases, building) these partnerships will be important to meeting longer-term strategic needs, as further explained below.

12. Empower individuals, neighborhoods, and communities to play a greater role throughout all phases of disasters. We know that regardless of the situation, the public will be involved, as first responders, as eyewitnesses, providing updates, serving as information nodes, or relaying critical information to authorities. Engagement with communities offers an opportunity to partner with individuals and organizations in life-saving and life-sustaining actions to strengthen their role in emergency management. The question is whether the emergency management community will

Strategic Foresight Initiative

succeed in building a constructive relationship with the public to empower them as a full partner in realizing mission success.

Why this need? There are real shifts underway in how people are processing information and how and where they will produce and consume it in the future. Additionally, there are corresponding shifts in the nature of trust, with public trust placed less in large organizations and increasingly in social networks. Along with these changes, the SFI scenarios depict a range of U.S. economic futures with spending constraints – especially over the next decade – as a repeated theme. Inevitably this will mean changes in how government services are delivered before, during, and after an emergency or disaster event. Understanding how to empower communities and individuals in new and different ways holds a critical key to enhancing our ability to achieve successful emergency management outcomes in the future; it also challenges our current public engagement approaches and expectations.

13. Proactively engage business in all emergency management phases *and* solicit its contribution to policy development, in light of the critical nature of private sector capabilities. We already engage the private sector in much of what we do. Moving forward, promoting further collaboration, cooperation, and appropriately close relationships between the private sector and the emergency management community will be vital. We will have to consider what legal and regulatory frameworks we will need in order to avoid conflicts of interest, since furthering our partnership with the private sector is a necessary element of serving the public in the future.

Providence, R.I., April 23, 2010 -- This advertising space, now being used for the FEMA phone number and web site, was donated on four digital billboards in Rhode Island to run PSAs on FEMA registration information. This is the digital sign along Route 10 in Cranston. Photo: Michael Rieger/FEMA

Figure 7: Providence, R.I., April 23, 2010

Why this need? The private sector meets the public's needs every day. With close to 90% of the labor force and tremendous specialized capabilities, the private sector is a key partner before, during, and after disasters. This partnership will become increasingly important in the future. Working in concert with the private sector, rather than competing with it, the public sector has an opportunity to further enable private sector resources and capabilities to assist in recovery efforts and resilience-building throughout communities. Engaging the private sector in policy development is also important so that the private sector has the appropriate frameworks in place to work effectively and cooperatively with the public sector to address issues of mutual concern.

Strategic Foresight Initiative

FEMA

14. Intensify disaster-response collaboration and planning with Canada and Mexico, recognizing scope for both national and local actions. Sharing critical emergency management information is a start to building collaborative cross-border relationships. As we do this, engaging the State Department and other authorities to ensure we have the appropriate agreements and frameworks in place will be important in the effort to intensify these relationships.

Why this need? Emergencies and disasters do not respect national boundaries. A number of the SFI scenarios anticipated the need for significantly closer U.S. collaboration with Canada and Mexico around several shared emergency management interest areas, including immigration, border security, drought and water management, disease surveillance, trade and commerce, and critical infrastructure. The scenarios made a strong case for anticipatory action to ensure the highest levels of cooperation are in place before actual emergencies or disasters occur.

---

15. Foster increased collaboration to ensure appropriate use of the military to provide specialized capabilities or to augment capacity in complex, overwhelming disaster incidents. This includes building on ties that already exist with respect to existing state and National Guard relationships. Strengthening dialogue between the military and local communities to coordinate resources and to foster trust and understanding will also be important. This is not uncharted territory, *per se*, but a new era of closer collaboration will be necessary.

Why this need? The SFI scenario discussions covered a range of complex emergency situations including weapons of mass destruction (WMDs), cyber attacks, and the potential need for quarantining pandemic victims showing up on U.S. shores. Responding to such threats will require scale, as well as specialized skills, some of which are within the purview of U.S. armed forces. If the U.S. reduces its global military footprint, the armed forces may be more available for domestic missions, including emergency management.

The strategic needs developed during the SFI scenario workshop process provide specifics into what we, as a community, should focus on in the coming decades to operate successfully in an evolving environment. These needs, like the drivers, are open to interpretation beyond the scenario workshop, and are not the exclusive set of needs we will have moving forward. However, they do provide a path we can follow as we begin to develop actions to meet all of our future needs. Envisioning the emergency management enterprise of the future, as we do in Section IV, will help bring life to the strategic needs and what we might do now to begin meeting them.

IV. A FUTURE GLIMPSE INTO EMERGENCY MANAGEMENT

The foresight process the SFI used systematically explored a range of plausible future scenarios and developed a set of common strategic needs that remain relevant no matter how the future unfolds. If one assumes for the moment that the emergency management community meets these needs, the future emergency management environment will look very different indeed. This section provides a glimpse of what the emergency management enterprise of 2030 might look like and how it might be mobilized to meet the identified strategic needs – essential capabilities it has developed, innovative models and tools it uses, and dynamic relationships and partnerships it has formed.

ESSENTIAL CAPABILITIES IN 2030

Emergency management professionals adopt emerging information and media channels to ensure an appropriate presence on new social media outlets. The emergency management community continuously pulls information from appropriate social networks, especially local discussions, and local internet news sources (e.g., Patch.com circa 2011) while simultaneously using these networks to push news and information out prior to and during disasters and emergencies. Emergency managers have access to private sector data and sensor networks relevant to their missions. They can locate, for example, remote populations that otherwise might not be identified. There are strong "need to share" protocols and memoranda of understanding (MOA) with all levels of government, especially federal authorities, and across national boundaries.

Volunteers serve in both operational and support emergency management roles. Databases contain pre-approved rosters of volunteer emergency management personnel with skills/qualifications. There is a *de facto* "professionalization" of volunteer corps with opportunities for advanced training, certification, and granting of appropriate authorities (medical, law enforcement, etc.). The emergency management community is leveraging the surge in baby boom retirement by creating meaningful volunteer opportunities, including important support roles (e.g., legal, communications, advocacy). For short-term response situations, the emergency management community is capable of providing quick and effective on-site/on-the-job training.

The education community has embraced emergency management as a focus of elementary and secondary education, similar to efforts in the last half of the 20th century around fire safety and prevention, personal safety, and safe driving. Elementary school children practice hands-on emergency management exercises. By high school graduation, each student can accurately identify numerous potential emergency situations and appropriate responses. Special training packages exist for each geographic region, focusing on major local threats such as tornadoes, hurricanes, floods, earthquakes, and forest fires.

Strategic Foresight Initiative

INNOVATIVE MODELS AND TOOLS IN 2030

A spirit of practical cooperation pervades emergency management leadership. States and municipalities have significantly fewer exclusive resources; emergency management people and assets are shared across borders to an unprecedented degree – and this includes some international jurisdictions (i.e., Canada and Mexico). This leads to well-defined, clear cross-border activity procedures and protocols, so that there is no question about access at the time of an emergency. There are new models for conducting emergency surge operations that take into account that there are far fewer redundancies in the nation's total national response and recovery assets. Credentials/qualifications of emergency management personnel are accepted across the U.S. (or at least within designated regions); personnel are more mobile.

The emergency management community has improved technological capabilities. Among them are risk-management and risk assessment tools that account for dynamic changes in hazard risks, such as climate change on flooding levels, and that anticipate interrelated and cascading effects of simultaneous multiple disasters and/or complex events. Emergency management planners take seriously a range of plausible multiple-event "scenarios," and they model the consequences of failure in one key infrastructure area for other key sectors (e.g., transportation, electricity, telecommunications, water, emergency services). As a result, vulnerable nodes are identified and rectified prior to an emergency or a disaster. An important feature of this is continual and sophisticated environmental scanning to understand the consequences of new and unfamiliar risks.

Unmanned Aerial Vehicles (UAVs) and robots provide powerful search and rescue capabilities. Pandemic sensors offer early warning of disease outbreaks. The emergency management community enjoys collaborative relationships with the technology community and even influences the development of emergency management applications. To make all this possible, coordination among emergency managers and a common set of standards to maximize interoperability and asset sharing has been incorporated into normal operations.

DYNAMIC PARTNERSHIPS IN 2030

Individuals and community institutions are further empowered and routinely contribute to emergency management. Local collective action is widespread as individuals and organizations (both formal and informal) assist in service delivery, survivor care, and community rebuilding efforts. Emergency management programs connect to communities through the social, economic, and political structures that are part of daily life. Public service announcements and community-based organizations articulate and continually reinforce what households should do across an appropriately wide range of short- and long-term situations, including natural disasters, WMD, terror events, disease outbreaks, and prolonged droughts and other environmental disasters.

Strategic Foresight Initiative

The emergency management community shares information with and gathers information from multiple media. In some cases, the emergency management community provides multilingual outreach to community groups and fraternal and faith-based organizations. In other cases, emergency managers and volunteers attend virtual neighborhood meetings as participants to learn what communities are doing. The emergency management community is active in social networks both as a producer and consumer of information.

The private sector contribution to emergency management has greatly expanded. Business leaders contribute actively to policy and planning activities, and participate in important emergency management boards and task forces. Emergency managers tap into private sector sensor nets (e.g., closed-circuit television cameras, and environmental and health sensors). Accomplished business professionals with emergency management-relevant skills (logistics, technology management, etc.) share their knowledge through special emergency management fellowships. Private sector volunteers are organized and trained to help during emergencies. To avoid legal and ethical problems, guidelines for private sector involvement in emergency management are well-defined, thus incentivizing expanded business roles and new forms of public-private cooperation. This includes small business at local community levels, as well as large, national enterprises.

Additionally, response models now reflect expanded use of National Guard (or state-sanctioned) forces and access to their facilities, equipment and technical skill sets. The availability of National Guard resources is more reliable as the U.S. reduces or is less expansive in its foreign military commitments. Emergency management personnel are trained to use military assets that are appropriate for emergency situations. Likewise, military personnel participate in routine emergency training exercises.

V. THE WAY FORWARD

The findings from the SFI process to date are as diverse as the communities that the SFI represents. The SFI cannot – nor did it ever intend to – provide detailed roadmaps for action. Each constituent community may decide what, from this large (and expanding) body of knowledge, is applicable to their region or community and what could be explored and acted upon. The strategic needs are useful catalysts for discerning priority areas for action, even if the first step on any single strategic need is a meaningful conversation with concerned stakeholders on how best to move forward on specific initiatives.

To meet its potential, the SFI must both actively engage new issues that will shape or affect emergency management, and expand participation in SFI research, dialogues, workshops, and other forums. Remaining alert to innovative new ideas and practices, and bringing foresight into the mainstream in our field, would greatly benefit the emergency management community.

A key part of the SFI mission is to advance a culture of "futures thinking" within the emergency management community that produces tangible benefits for the community. By revisiting and refining our collective understanding of the future and our needs, and through building a shared sense of direction and urgency to meet those needs, we set ourselves on a dynamic path. The SFI will continue to engage the emergency management community and those it serves, both in-person and virtually, to continue research on important trends and drivers, and to explore policy and planning options and implications.

Since early 2010 the SFI work has uncovered insights that challenge, refine, and in many cases validate current discussions occurring throughout the emergency management community. Fortunately, some have already begun taking actions to meet the needs of future environments, and a broad cross-section of the emergency management community has been engaged to raise awareness and understanding of what the future could hold. However, we can and must do more today in order to set a positive trajectory for our community in meeting future needs. While the exact future form of the SFI will evolve over time, it will involve several key components including:

- Refreshing and expanding the research to explore new and compelling questions and ideas;
- Developing useful products to distribute throughout the community (e.g., reports and trend analyses);
- Aligning strategies and planning selected actions to meet future needs; and
- Continuing to engage stakeholders to broaden the SFI community and build on existing collaboration.

The SFI is a work in progress and not intended to serve as the final word on what the future will hold, what we will face, or how to approach pending changes. The process has, however, provided an opportunity to engage the broad emergency management community and ask: "Is what we are doing now sufficient to meet our future needs?" and "How might we change our approaches and mindsets?" Additionally, the SFI process highlights the need to expand this discussion further, throughout the whole emergency management community – beyond disciplines and across sectors – to enable the collaboration that produces effective emergency management outcomes today and in the future.

To get involved in the SFI, send an email to FEMA-OPPA-SFI@fema.gov and request to be included in the SFI Community. You will receive access to updated newsletters and SFI events. You also will be informed about new materials and blog postings and are invited to respond and engage in the discussion.

Visit our Web site to learn about the SFI, read the driver research papers, and see our blog section if you are interested in commenting on our work -
http://www.fema.gov/about/programs/oppa/strategic_foresight_initiative.shtm

APPENDIX A–THE SFI PROCESS

The SFI Process consists of three primary steps: Environmental Scanning, Scenario Planning, and Advancing and Sustaining Foresight. The diagram below depicts the corresponding activities for each step.

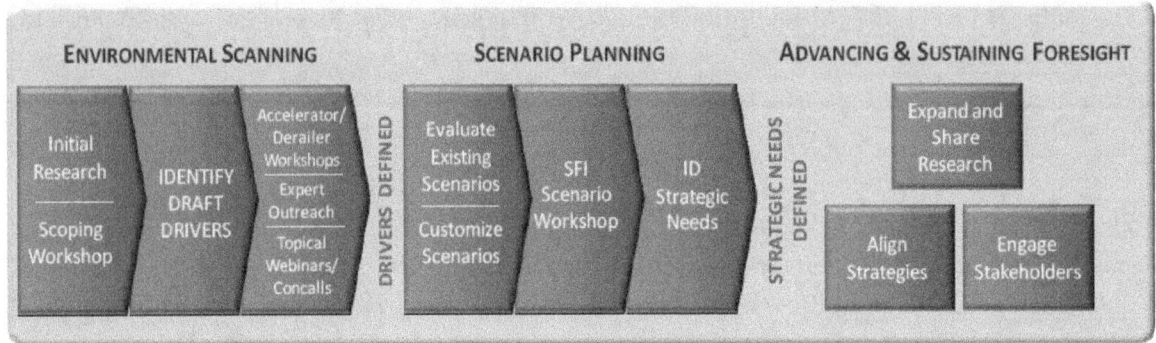

Environmental Scanning

Initial Research

The process began in December 2009 when the SFI engaged emergency management community stakeholders to fashion a research agenda of factors that will drive and shape the future environment. The SFI team began this initial research and literature analysis by reviewing several future methodologies and literature on broad topic areas that could shape the future. These areas included sociology and demographics, politics, technology, climate change, economics, security and terrorism.

The literature review included the following:

- "Global Trends 2025" – the National Intelligence Council
- "Project Horizon" – Various US Government Agencies
- "Project Evergreen" – US Coast Guard
- "Energy Scenarios to 2050" – Shell Oil Company
- "Forces That Will Shape America's Future" – Government Accountability Office
- "15 Global Challenges" – The Millennium Project
- " Joint Operating Environment" – US Joint Forces Command
- "QHSR "Security Environment" – Department of Homeland Security
- National Intelligence Strategy "Strategic Environment" – Office of the Director of National Intelligence
- "Global Strategic Assessment 2009" – Institute for National Strategic Studies

To gain additional insights and opinions on these topic areas, the SFI team conducted individual and group discussions with subject matter experts to substantiate the initial research and to broaden the SFI's focus. The SFI team's research, review and consultation on the issues identified as shaping the future led to a clearer understanding of the stakeholders the SFI would need to engage. These stakeholders are considered to be the "Emergency Management Community." This community includes, but is not limited to, the following: traditional state, local, federal, and tribal emergency managers; those in public security, public health, and public safety agencies; first responders; public works; business partners; non-governmental organizations (NGOs); federal agencies with equities in emergency management; and academicians who have studied or published on the topic of emergency management.

Scoping Workshop

Based on the initial research and literature review, in April 2010 the SFI team held a Scoping Workshop in Washington, DC to identify, define, and refine key issues and drivers that may affect the future of emergency management. To obtain a wide cross-section of perspectives and expertise, workshop participants included 30 persons encompassing the spectrum of the Emergency Management Community. The efforts of this workshop led to the identification of nine drivers likely to shape change and significantly affect the field of emergency management over the next fifteen to twenty years.

The nine drivers identified at the Scoping Workshop are detailed in <u>Appendix B</u>.

Outreach, Workshops, Webinars

Through outreach and engagement efforts, the SFI team built an SFI community of nearly 800 individuals. The nine drivers became the focus of the community's work. Dialogue on the drivers was conducted through conference calls, webinars, additional workshops, and an online discussion. These discussions created greater understanding of how the drivers might evolve and interact to shape the future environment.

2010 – 2011 Workshops

The workshops either attended or hosted by the SFI to further inform SFI research and outreach efforts include:

- **Inter-Agency Board (IAB) – Strategic Planning Sub-Group (October 2010; February 2011; May 2011)**: The IAB is a voluntary collaborative panel of emergency preparedness and response practitioners from a wide array of professional disciplines that represent all levels of government and the voluntary sector. The SFI team first engaged the IAB Strategic Planning Sub-Group (SPSG) in October 2010 to provide a project overview. In ensuing meetings held in February 2011 and May 2011, the SFI team provided project updates and sought insights used to customize scenarios for the SFI Scenario Workshop held in July 2011.

- **National Defense University, Washington, DC (February 15, 2011)**: FEMA, in conjunction with the National Defense University, convened 13 subject matter experts for a full-day workshop to discuss trends that are shaping how individuals relate to society. The experts included government officials, first responders, and academics. They provided their perspectives about the trends affecting individuals, research about changes in our society, and actions to consider in response to those changes.

- **Young Professionals Workshops, Washington, DC (February 22 & 28, 2011)**: To obtain input to the SFI from a broader age range of individuals, the SFI team held two workshops to gain insights from young professionals. Approximately 25 persons, mainly working in the Department of Homeland Security (DHS) and FEMA, participated in the workshops. Information gathered from these workshops informed the customization of scenarios for the SFI Scenario Workshop.

- **FOCUS Symposium, Brussels, Belgium (May 2011)**: The Center for European Security Studies invited the SFI team to give a presentation at its FOCUS Symposium. Through the FOCUS Project, the European Union (EU) seeks input from stakeholders from within and beyond the EU on the employment of foresight as a tool to address EU security needs and challenges. The SFI team provided an overview of SFI and explained how engaging in foresight to understand trends can prepare us to get ahead of those trends before they become "strategic surprises."

- **Actionable Foresight Work Program, National Defense University, Washington, DC (May – July 2011)**: Team members attended a series of workshops at NDU on Actionable Foresight and Anticipatory Governance hosted by The Project on Forward Engagement. At these events, representatives from government and academia met to discuss proposals to institutionalize foresight in governance in order to detect trends that may affect our society. Governments could then use that knowledge to create policies to address challenges.

Driver Research Papers Fiscal Year 2010 - 2011

The SFI team combined information gleaned from outreach activities with additional research on the drivers and created research papers on each of the nine driver topics. To ensure maximum dissemination and spur additional discussion, the papers were posted on the SFI Website and the FEMA Blog where they can be viewed and downloaded by both specialists and the public at large. The driver paper synopses and Web links are located in Appendix B of this report.

Scenario Planning

Scenario planning is used by both government and the private sector to investigate possible futures and to integrate appropriate actions into strategic and operational planning. The SFI used scenario planning to help participants extend their analytical understanding of the future and to assist them in examining a range of plausible future operating conditions. This examination helped to guide relevant policy and actions for the participants. The US Coast Guard has engaged in scenario planning since 1998 and made available its newly developed *Project Evergreen* scenarios as a resource for the SFI. The SFI used these scenarios as a baseline, integrated them with the 18 months of research and community input, and produced five SFI-relevant scenarios or "worlds" that more closely mirror the drivers and uncertainties of the future operating environment. These scenarios were used in the first SFI Scenario Workshop in July 2011.

SFI Scenario Workshop, Washington, DC (July 2011)

The purpose of this workshop was to explore confluences of the nine drivers among the five plausible future worlds and use them to determine what the future may hold and how we can prepare to meet future challenges. The SFI workshop scenarios were detailed, systematically developed descriptions of operating environments that emergency management might face over the next fifteen to twenty years. Each participant was assigned to one of the five worlds. The nearly 60 workshop participants were instructed to use their judgment and expertise to address emergency management needs and concerns in the world to which they were assigned. Their efforts ultimately resulted in the identification of 15 stress-tested *strategic needs* divided into three categories: (1) Essential Capabilities the community will need to build or enhance; (2) Innovative Models and Tools emergency managers will need to create or utilize; and (3) Dynamic Partnerships that will need to be formed or strengthened.

Strategic Foresight Initiative

SFI Scenario Worlds Synopses

In **Bet on the Wrong Horse**, a decade-long cycle of extreme weather prompted widespread acceptance that anthropogenic (human-caused) dramatic climate changes were occurring. New data suggests the previous climate-warming trend has in fact stopped. Expected coastal erosion and rapid sea-level rise has not come to pass. After massive investment in renewable energy sources and climate engineering, many speculate as to whether the U.S. has bet on the wrong horse. Although this bet has led to improvements in pollution and spurred research and development, the U.S. economy is bobbing in and out of recessions.

In **Dragon vs. Tiger**, the U.S. is a good place to live and work. Every day the media focuses on the continuing tensions between China and India, which, although troubling, has not yet erupted into open conflict. The U.S. has certainly benefitted - the U.S. economy has rebounded and is moderately strong, we are once again the global leader in technology and attracting business. But lurking beneath what is in many respects a positive world for the U.S. is the risk of complacency.

In **Dude, Where's My Sovereignty** the U.S. is a gloomy place. An endless series of incompetent and uncompromising governments failed to arrive at anything comprehensive to fund the Baby Boom retirements and maintain fiscal sanity. Our global influence has waned, and because the federal government is seen as ineffectual and underfunded, states do many things that used to be strictly federal responsibility. All are worse off than they were a few decades ago. Globally, international business elites and a few countries exert influence to avoid seemingly inevitable resource-extraction anarchy in the global commons.

In **Quantum Leap,** the U.S. is enjoying a renaissance. A technological revolution fostered by aggressive public-private investment has given the U.S. bleeding-edge advantages in computing, nanotechnology, smart materials, and robotics. But it's not all upside. The world struggles with the increasingly destructive effects of global climate change. Oil-producing economies will soon be on the brink of collapse, a globally networked "elite" appears to enjoy superior political and economic advantages, and cybercrime and intellectual property theft are rampant. No one knows where this brave new cyber world will lead, but for now Americans are enjoying the best economy since the 1990s.

In **Treading Water** the U.S. is very much a changed country as it deals with long-term stagnation bordering on depression. Unemployment is chronically high, and meaningful recovery does not appear imminent. It is a time of self-reliance and community focus. The nation has grown notably more insulated and pragmatic in global affairs, yet relations with Mexico and Canada have never been more important. A series of deadly pandemics has swept the globe and reinforced rising protectionist and isolationist sentiments. Military spending in the U.S. has been scaled back. U.S. homeland security roles have been increasingly redefined around disease management, border security and emergency response. Environmental regulations have been mostly shelved, in this austere national setting.

Advancing and Sustaining Strategic Foresight

The hope is the emergency management community will employ the 15 strategic needs to inform how we move forward as a community. Since April 2010, the SFI has focused on understanding who or what could shape the future of emergency management, and on identifying our strategic needs as we face this complex and uncertain future. While the exact future form of the SFI will evolve, it will involve several key components, including:

- Refreshing and expanding the research to explore new and compelling questions and ideas;
- Developing useful products to distribute throughout the community (e.g., reports and trend analyses);
- Aligning strategies and planning selected actions to meet future needs; and
- Continuing to engage stakeholders to broaden the SFI community and build on existing collaboration.

To help accomplish the bulleted activities listed above, the SFI team has reached out to members of the emergency management community since the July 2011 SFI Scenario workshop. We are engaging the community to "socialize" the SFI findings, gather feedback and reactions, identify questions and issues to examine in future research, and explore ways to utilize current work. Prior to publication of this report, the team shared SFI findings with the following groups at conferences and workshops they have hosted:

- Local, State, Tribal, and Federal Preparedness Task Force (September 2011)
- The National Advisory Council (September 2011)
- National Association of Emergency Managers (October 2011)
- Inter-Agency Board (November 2011)
- International Association of Emergency Managers (November 2011)
- George Washington University Homeland Security Policy Institute (December 2011)

APPENDIX B–SFI DRIVERS

The SFI team combined information gleaned from outreach activities with additional research on the drivers and created research papers on each of the nine driver topics. To ensure maximum dissemination and spur additional discussion, the papers were posted on the SFI website and the FEMA Blog where they could be viewed and downloaded by both specialists and the public at large. Direct links to each of the driver papers are listed below each driver description:

Social and Technological Drivers:

- *Technological Innovation and Dependency.* The pace of growth of new technologies—from biotechnology and nanotechnology to information and communication technology—is accelerating, and affecting nearly every facet of life. Smartphones, high-speed Internet, and "cloud" computing, to name only a few examples, are transforming business, how people communicate, and essential services such as health care. Conversely, the ubiquity of technology is exposing new risks: dependence on computer systems to manage operations in multiple sectors, such as water, telecommunications, and transportation infrastructure, increases vulnerabilities, including the threat of cyber attacks.
  http://www.fema.gov/pdf/about/programs/oppa/technology_dev_%20paper.pdf

- *Changing Role of the Individual.* Technological innovation and the public's evolving expectations of government could lead to a redefinition of community beyond geography and nationality, fundamentally changing how individuals interact with society. New tools have empowered the public to play a greater role in identifying "what matters" (e.g., by broadcasting news stories through their networks) and producing content themselves (e.g., eyewitness videos captured on cell phones). Social networks, rather than traditional institutions or experts, are becoming more trusted and influential in peoples' daily lives.
  http://www.fema.gov/pdf/about/programs/oppa/changing_role_individual.pdf

- *Universal Access to and Use of Information.* Evolving patterns of information flow have changed the role of the media and modes of information exchange. The explosion of social media and personal communications technology will continue to increase real-time access and delivery of information. Public access to "raw" data sources, such as Data.gov, expands the possibilities of how existing information can be used, and increases expectations of government transparency. The volume of available information, however, is creating a "data deluge" and making it difficult for individuals to filter and know what is important.
  http://www.fema.gov/pdf/about/programs/oppa/universal_access_paper_051011.pdf

- *U.S. Demographics Shifts.* The U.S. population is growing, aging significantly and becoming more ethnically diverse. These are transformative trends: by 2025, as immigration continues to fuel the majority of population growth, nearly 1 in 5 Americans will be older

32

than 65. People are residing in more densely populated urban and coastal areas, which may be more vulnerable to impacts from severe weather. These trends will create new medical, cultural, and linguistic challenges that affect critical planning, response, and recovery functions across the fields of emergency management.

http://www.fema.gov/pdf/about/programs/oppa/demography_%20paper_051011.pdf

Environmental Driver:

- *Climate Change.* Per the U.S. Global Change Research Program (USGCRP) study on the implications of climate change in the United States: coastal areas will be at risk due to rising sea levels and more intense storms; domestic and global water resources will be stressed; there will be new threats to human health; and wild land fire threats will increase and shift to previously unaffected areas. Aging critical infrastructure and increased urban populations could exacerbate climate change challenges, while mass migration due to climate issues, increased conflict, and shifts in disease patterns are potential international effects of climate change.

  http://www.fema.gov/pdf/about/programs/oppa/climate_change_paper.pdf

Economic and Political Drivers:

- *Global Interdependencies / Globalization.* In recent decades, globalization has improved international socioeconomic conditions while creating new global interdependencies that will influence emergency management. While improved living standards may yield greater community resilience to disasters, inadequate institutional capacity and deepening regional ties may result in greater demand for U.S. assistance in international disaster relief. Moreover, America's reliance on an increasingly vulnerable global supply chain and shifting international power dynamics may also mean that catastrophes abroad have a greater impact domestically.

  http://www.fema.gov/pdf/about/programs/oppa/global_interdependencies.pdf

- *Government Budgets.* Near- and medium-term forecasts show serious constraints for state, local, and federal budgets. Even over the long term, state and municipal budgets are projected to require significant realignment to better contain costs/spending and increase revenues. Diminished resources, increasing health care costs, and the costs of retirement benefits will likely impact emergency managers directly and indirectly at all levels of government for years to come, raising questions about the role of federal, state, local, and tribal entities in emergency management.

  http://www.fema.gov/pdf/about/programs/oppa/government_budgets_paper.pdf

- *Critical Infrastructure.* Aging transportation, communication, energy and health care infrastructure pose significant threats and are in danger of failing over the next 15-20 years. Collapsing bridges, bursting water mains, cascading brownouts from a fragile power grid,

and overburdened health and medical systems are all examples of this well documented situation. Without reliable infrastructure in place, protection, response, and recovery operations may suffer.

http://www.fema.gov/pdf/about/programs/oppa/critical_infrastructure_paper.pdf

- *Evolving Terrorist Threat.* The availability of technological and scientific knowledge has the potential to transform both terrorist and counterterrorist capabilities. The rapidly evolving information environment, meanwhile, continues to create avenues for individuals and small groups to seek out and associate with extremists. Global terrorist organizations are adopting new tactics (e.g., cyber terrorism), while the threat of homegrown terrorist activity continues to grow. The changing dynamics of national and international security will affect the Nation's safety, prosperity, and resilience.

http://www.fema.gov/pdf/about/programs/oppa/evolving_terrorist_threat.pdf

*Strategic
Foresight Initiative*

APPENDIX C – SFI PARTICIPATING ORGANIZATIONS

The organizations listed below were represented during at least one SFI workshop conducted from March 2010-September 2011 and/or during individual interviews that explored the impacts and implications of the nine identified drivers on the emergency management community. This is not an exhaustive list of all individuals and organizations that have participated in SFI to date.

American Public Works Association
Arizona State University
Arlington County (VA) Office of Emergency
  Management
Arlington County Virginia
Association of State and Territorial Health
  Officials
Bellevue, WA Fire Department
Big City Emergency Managers, Inc.
Brandon University – Canada
Buncombe County (NC) Health Department
Business Executives for National Security
California Polytechnic State University
Center for European Union Security Studies
Center for National Policy
Center for Strategic and International Studies
Community and Regional Resilience Institute
Cunningham (CO) Fire Protection District
Disaster Research Center
Disaster Resilience Leadership Academy,
  Tulane University
Disasters Roundtable, The National
  Academies
District of Columbia Homeland Security and
  Emergency Management Agency
Elmira College
Emergency Management Academy of New
  Zealand
Emergency Management Magazine
Exponent
Federal Bureau of Investigation
Federal Emergency Management Agency
Frederick County (MD) Division of
  Emergency Management
Frederick County (MD) Sheriff's Office
George Mason University Center for
  Transportation and Economic Development
George Washington University
Georgetown University

Gloucester County (NJ) Office of Emergency
  Management
Homeland Security Institute
Howard County Maryland
Incident
Indiana Department of Homeland Security
Inter-Agency Board
International Association of Chiefs of Police
International Association of Emergency
  Managers
Iowa Homeland Security and Emergency
  Management Division
Islamic Relief USA
Jacksonville State University
Journal of Homeland Security and Emergency
  Management
Las Vegas Metropolitan Police Department
Lawrence Livermore National Laboratory
Massachusetts Institute of Technology
Methodist University
National Academies of Science
National Association of City and County
  Health Officials
National Association of Counties
National Association of Development
  Organizations
National Association of Home Builders
National Baptist Convention, USA Inc.
National Conference of State Legislatures
National Defense University
National Disability Rights Network
National Disaster Management Institute,
  Korea
National Emergency Management Association
National Governors Association
National Guard Bureau
National Intelligence Council
National League of Cities
National Oceanic and Atmospheric
  Administration

National Science Foundation
National Sheriffs' Association
New York City Fire Dept
Newton Emergency Management
North Dakota State University
Oregon Emergency Management Agency
Pennsylvania Emergency Management
  Agency
Pennsylvania State University
Pennsylvania State University – Harrisburg
Pew Research Center
Prospect Heights (IL) Fire Protection District
Pueblo of Tesuque Tribe
State of Wisconsin, Department of Military
  Affairs
STG International
Target Corporation
The Brookings Institution
The Jewish Federations of North America
The National Advisory Council

U. S. Capitol Police
U. S. Census Bureau
U.S. Conference of Mayors
U.S. Department of Defense
U.S. Department of Health and Human
  Services
U.S. Department of Homeland Security
U.S. Department of Transportation
United State Coast Guard
United States Air Force
University of Colorado – Boulder
University of Delaware
University of Houston
University of Maryland Baltimore County
University of Maryland University College
University of North Carolina at Pembroke
University of Oklahoma
University of Richmond
University of South Florida
Witt & Associates

Strategic
Foresight Initiative

FEMA

www.ingramcontent.com/pod-product-compliance
Lightning Source LLC
Chambersburg PA
CBHW080346290526
45791CB00009BA/2764